To LRS

For giving me permission to do it all

Table of Contents

One

A Brief History of Hysteria   1

Are You Normal Tonight?   3

First World   4

Post-immaculate   6

Getting to Know You   7

And This is Rare   9

The Sheets and Sun Are Soft and Good But This Isn't Food Enough   10

Telekinesis   11

After the Ceremony   12

The Moon Can't Drag a Thing   13

Singles   14

We Are Married   15

I Am a Found Thing Now   16

Hagiography   17

Catastrophe   18

Thanksgiving Dinner   20

Two

Dark Horoscope   23

Ambassadors to Our Own Delight   24

Bottle of Blues   25

The Milk of It   26

Everybody's Knife Bible   27

Portrait in Flat   28

Elizabeth   29

American Cosmology   30

Irrefutable Evidence   31

The Projected Future Has Been Cancelled   32

Dreaming the Places My Father's Tongue Has Been in Summer   33

Theorem   34

Adolescence   35

But I Will Carve Your Name Into Any Tree Like I Am Fourteen
And Do Not Know What Darkness is Possible   36

Knickerbocker Avenue   37

Three

Irresistible Empire — 41

Stand By Your Man — 42

Sisters — 43

Your Mother: Franz Kafka. My Father: A Hole Ripped in the Night. — 44

Far as Fieldstones from Our Heads — 45

Intimacy — 46

Soft Volcano — 47

Wedding Season — 48

In Every Lonely Place, An Alter — 49

Sheriff Teeth — 50

Green Hour — 51

Small Rooms — 52

Where God Was Not — 53

Convince Me Eternity — 55

"And least will guess that with our bones
We left much more, left what still is
The look of things, left what we felt"

—Wallace Stevens, "A Postcard from the Volcano"

One

A Brief History of Hysteria

All of this magic is death:

> your vicious little organ singing like a drunk uncle,

> the beautiful, white-headed children

> that passed through your body,

the cats you fed till plump as pimples and languid.

Who let the rot in? And what if you never return—full and free—

> to that alleyway in Morocco where old men watched
> as he entered you?

Where are your daughters?

> The holiday pies filled blood-red with wild rhubarb.

And tonight, on each continent, women are teaching other women to be vessels.
Women are singing sweetly to get what they want by force.

What will you remember of this place?

> The naked limbs in the orchard,

> the crust left along the empty bowl,

your own hands on your stomach in the browned-out night.

A sense of abandon placed among the linen, sharp-lined and never dirty.

On gray gadgets you're kept humming.

Stories about rivers are stories about girls who want things, you taught them.
    And the machines that fix other machines are not glamorous technologies.

In the yellow kitchen, a silent anxiety attack.

    Breathe deep and drop nothing off your tray, my sweet.

Are You Normal Tonight?

The arterial beauty of Florida is alive in all of its obesity.
And the sequin sellers are doing good business
east of Granada Boulevard.

*

The sad-eyed woman's ultrasound image—all dirty blur of gray and ambiguous
genitalia—sits lovingly electric on your newsfeed.

And the neighbor with his disorder you invented is going out tonight.

*

The starlet will eat a sandwich and Kevin will push the joke
too far—the vomit, the bobby pins—
and that's okay tonight.

*

And your mother, with her rough hands, her quiet advice, has walked
along the sidewalk knowing how cold a wooden house can feel

wondering whose soft, strange lips she could kiss.

First World

The West was an un-storied mound my mother rose out of. It was a backlit mountain
and cold stove at dawn my father rode toward in the beginning of his adult life

from a clapboard place called Ridgefield. Nineteen sixty-eight or nine, and her hair
was longer than the road to Flagstaff, her eyes brown as broken ground.

A train took them back east, and I was born under an organized sky in the arms of fences
and small birds. My sister came with pretty hands like orchard peaches and eyes

like passing through a forest toward home. In late light, I met a man but was unable
to tell him, I *like you in sentences and on fire*, knowing only to take off the words

like a blouse. Why did we enter the story like this? My mother couldn't articulate
the small coffin they laid the body of the neighbor girl inside. That is it. That will always

be it. How wrong to ask for the gift of a little grief. I'll say a cold prayer for the knives
whining in the drawer, for my sister's yellow head asleep at my feet instead.

I have seen the ruthlessness of skys cut open, the devastating nothing of some men,
and the sweet heavy brow of a few good ones. In the season of steam coating the air,

and of cracks rising in cups, I think my sister may be the only breathing thing formed
of wings. My mother and I, we have different types of ghosts. Out of the grand mouth

of the dirty kitchen sink in morning light, I see the loved world is not far away, and we
are more than a tiny stirring of strings. There is nothing less difficult than that. No secret

outside of town, no bruise-painted lip, no stained sheets to fold, to put away. Just the ache of the tiniest gestures, the tanned calf of my father, the steely face of Flatirons, rising

to drink coffee at dawn. Born to a world of coin and book, our faces are broken by blue. My sister eats the best of them like dust, while in my quiet mouth rests an open hand.

Post-immaculate

It's not what you think.

A young man came like Sunday morning,
showed me a little of myself. Now

my father is breaking where he folds and further. I am older
on account of Sunday morning and his hairless legs.

Time puts a little scorch on the body,
the marks of which are dark masts sailing on the ocean
of the long, slow unfolding of a small terrible.

What more: the skirmish of hair beneath his hands.
There is no body I despise like my own.

But I have one black fight left. And I see you there,
wet with the light of the moon,
And my family, and something like god.

They are patient little owls
asleep in the limbs of the sycamore tree.

Getting to Know You

I could pursue a degree in the erotics of his knee peeking hungrily from frays.
Tee-shirt soft as ice cream.
As soon as I learned it, I forget his egregious middle name.

*

A khaki heart breaks like any other.
But there is not one innocent thing he told me.
In the small church of his childhood, I was the errant alter boy.

*

Gift of a little belly caught among button, in belt.
What this small flesh summons.
Below his neck, scent of hot streets after rain.

*

Pants whispered along his crotch as he walked.
So many boxes of shoes.
There was both a bending over and spaghetti alla carbonara.

*

And when he cried, I wanted him less.
Clean denim like an apology crushed to the floor.
I must resist the urge to fold them.

*

I wish to live within the warm muggy cavern of Diadora,
in the evening by the oak trees after practice.
The lemons on the counter. The keys finding their hook.

And This is Rare

My name means a promise, one made to God. And where
is your mother tonight? Her head like old leaves left in the yard.

Before I knew you, each night I would walk under the orange-bellied limbs,
past the ratty houses and toward the brick set, solid as love.

We are at the point where we need sympathy and a little more blood.
Trust me when I say everyone you care about has committed a crime.

The overturned oyster shells were smoke caught in a sunset
over some Asian city we'll never see. The wine like every glass of wine.

I started to love you because you could list the things that make you tremble
on your hand. But tonight the moon wears a blue suit, and somewhere nearby

someone is laughing. The restaurant down the street is almost empty.
The woman at the bar clings to her own beautiful hair.

The Sheets and Sun Are Soft and Good But This Isn't Food Enough

A clot of dark in your mother's neck is making her sick.
You will lift your head from this pillow each day
and pay to make her bright where you can.

It's true: people who joke about money
don't need more money.

And in the morning, the air around you
is peach sweet and heavy.
You kick through the night, the bed dirty with dream.
The pigeons wait and wait and come like late stones.

Your mother dreams like a dog
on another island.

If this room were a kingdom, all noble power
would reside in your fingers
and in the softness of your eyelids.
That bagged flesh like love.

Telekinesis

The bruise of a couch and the woman I will never love are at it again tonight.

History's little edge has me lit up like San Antonio.

Days go limp, bent over the bedroom chair and begging.
The grey hut of these hands resigned.

Like clockwork, river fingers are sick with impulse.

The bars are drained, but the Kitchen Aids whir and spin.

Some lips are cracked, some are stained.

And I wonder at the mouths of pigs,

those museum hallways of hunger, pink-lit, wet and regal.

After the Ceremony

Earlier, it was the yeasty smell of hopper legs and field lust.

The strange neighbors rising to smoke behind ivy.

While in the made bed of our undoing, a small animal reclined, sliced open.
You were eating berries by the door.

It was obvious that this picnic was a disaster. Not one thing could be solved
with rough-mouthed crumpets.

Leave your cereal, they said. Leave the wooden picture frame.
All the empty lobster tanks will find a home.

The Moon Can't Drag a Thing

The sky nearly lickable in its buffed blackness.

You've brought yourself to this relaxing addendum.
Now you must gather the wettest pieces in your eyes.

Nature, that tiny mindfuck. That nymph-maker. The sop
of some lonesome steel guitar among the twitchy pines.

Scent of a field giving it up to the besotted atmosphere.
And this lake yearning to be combed, hungry for lost bracelet, lost body,

with its small swell of danger, indelible smoke stain on tidy cumuli.

Singles

He was built of beauty marks; I was in the openness of post-cruelty,
had read the internet that morning.

Done with ghost hair and reason,
the dark decency,
the system with its soft openings.

Money and the scent a daylong body weeps. Sleep like a dress put on.
I had fixed my teeth and stopped with the meat,

thinking I could blend in rich.

The day turned night, turned linen then. Fat with wet all over.

We Are Married

And have been as lonely as the crusted shoreline.
That soft craw holding disaster, your sweating hands, the sunlight
still undulant and visible.

Replace the milk with white goodness and find a less difficult way to say this.
A dead child is my unnamed god, dusty as a pantry.

In the wake of all we have experienced: the broken glasses, the annihilated
expectations the color of mother's sensible bob,
do you still believe—

The market demands sinew and soft gloss, delicate breads at midnight.

To me, you were always a phone booth in a field. Even here,
even now, the Dutch oven like a singing bowl—all pelvis, all gaping and open.

I Am a Found Thing Now

This rawness against asphalt
completes the new curve of me.

Wanting to be fattened on air,
my sky was peeled away

and the prize: a slight terror
falling like small rain.

Beneath a little halo of
grotesquerie, I am visited

by phantom flight, hollow
as a clapperless bell. Far off

and half-functioning the weightless
machine of me flies.

Hagiography

Gently brush the fuzz
crowning your delicate arms
in a single direction.
Eat a red fruit sensuously.

Realize the molecules are temporary.
They will rearrange in time.
Drink until you reach the point of death
and you feel otherworldly.

Do not drink at all.
Masturbate continuously on a Sunday.

Study images of flawless women.
Do not listen to good music.
Build a cathedral of tears and money.

Have a sense of humor
about how hungry you are, but not about

how angry you are. Read the classics
and do not forget
to brush your teeth
because the details will become unbearable.

Catastrophe

Under the covers, discover a pile of hurts,
socks, and the shakes.

But for now, darkness is a shirt.

The man on the corner hollering to heartache

                knows a thing or two about me.

So does the woman,

         all crumpled housedress and tits,

growing like a tired flower

         from the second story window

above DeKalb Avenue.

          All of us just trying to slip quietly into the soft place.

I have mourned the heap of little failures in my future.
As usual, left ragamuffin unawares.

Home is spent and the evening:

           short, insipid, purple. Seeking all the ways to reach

          thirty-seven unscathed.

On a gently lit day, Heaven will not be spotted.
Heaven is 5:17 PM. It is the lip of gold on the vase. The ice. The bells.

       Assemble the kills like small rocks smoothed by ocean. Do not call
    them by name.
And in this way, the pistol of your lips is not something I fear.

Though my broke throat yells guttural:

       this is the most penultimate I have appeared in years.

Thanksgiving Dinner

The pills lay scattered like tiny meals across the countertop.

What is left to do but ravish

the long work,

a small heaven between fingers and the road to what—

when I say Joycean and everyone seated at the table agrees.

I cannot sleep with this wounded up head.

We've stocked the cabinets with bad news, called the wooden floors luxurious.

My mother sits like a basket of apples in the sun,

that little guru. My father a wolf still.

Tonight the bowled sky cracked and leaked through the smaller hours.
And somehow I thought the deeper we wandered,

the stranger and more beautiful the haze would become.

Two

Dark Horoscope

My father in his moonface: what thirty tedious years of work built.

Mountains rest in their slow gray curve, a velvet blanket of poplars poured over top.

These things are warm coin in a cold hand,
as the sick sun bobs around a far shore of trees: hard, plastic, and real.

Spindly fingers of rivers stretch along the hills, as though securing them in place,
imposing a wet grip on the land. Tiny chokehold and old whiff of fire.

How many men have died face up in a field in this corridor of Virginia. How many
have confused small things for love.

        The snakes in the woodpile do not fault us for our technology.

The grouse on the road ambles along.

        All blades are singing here. Their mouths wide open.

Ambassadors to Our Own Delight

Every month is April now, as though our situation had merited the word
emergency, but no one told us which jacket to wear. No one mentioned the weather,
that the pulsing evening would contain both lilacs and bird death.
But now we've named our hearts after animals,
Though the mission has grown obscure.
But the feelings, they have become solid, more like real furniture.

Bottle of Blues

The little god of elsewhere eyes is quiet tonight
as I occupy myself with earthly things. Outside heaven
pants and TVs glow celestially with old news.

All morning the sky was a wool bath, edges of buildings gone fuzzy,
trees and children vague.
These days I am taming the feral love of distances.
The weird lust of the everyday.
Soothing the hook of sleep with the beauty of small pharmaceuticals.

I say "these days" to set them apart from the staggering importance
of those days because the now is never suitable.
The humming lights of now will never do.

The Milk of It

eanwhile, my mother's heart set a-humming,
wet with worship and fatigue.
It's the temple of her body I disregard.
Would if she could plant a seed.
Would if I could cut out the middle man.
And how time rounds us
of our pointed corners,
we grow weighted with dusks,
with irons and silks.
How we slowly learn the ways we are,
delicately, delightfully,
not exceptional at all.

Everybody's Knife Bible

Lips rest on a piece of slick meat before it enters the mouth.
Outside, the falling sun shines like a sheep's eye.

Death will not be held off,
not with these fists of black flies.

In the yard, a man wraps palm trees in plastic for winter
as small explosions recline in the dark.

Apparently, this is our project: carefully
tracing the curve of a chin in blue light.

The finer knives sleep in elaborate cases.
Even unimportant decisions can be unmade.

Portrait in Flat

Like the plane, horizon's reality
running through the bloody mess
of sundown, we're flat. Sure,

we walk upright, admiring watch-faces
in the jewelry store. Poor girdled time,
nowhere to go but straight
and out. Happenstance places us

perpendicular, at odds with the ground.
No use denying you're a name on a page,
page in a book on the forest floor
flush as the impenetrable surface

of cold coffee. And yet
you flatten the Chinese lantern
and there is light in it still.

Elizabeth

An orange-jacketed morning has let me loose over the clean,
        cat-tailed collar bone of New Jersey in a slick purposeful bus.
Then the memory of your face bent by wind,
        as though parts of it were wishing to be somewhere else that night.

Remember the telephone? That sleek black animal. Remember a letter,
        which meant things would never be the same. Now clouds are livid
with light-licked dirt and the sensation of not belonging.
        The day drench and the languor,

is the narrow hope sucked clean out of space with the dark, smoky force
        of your own tongue. But trust me: it's as simple as wanting it in you, rather
than over there. I believe beauty is in the long want, the hot chase,
        in under-lit parking lots, small disappointments

stacked up like coins. Beauty is in that old ingenious song of the heart.
        Little fang of light over Paterson: I am pinning a lot on you,
what sustains with the particular tincture of inner thigh, in flex and hair.
        I am certain someday the craved world will be the one I am living in.

American Cosmology

My mother pressed eight plum-sized lungs
into this unforgiving world
but she failed each one. Or they did. Or she did.
Then she hefted the wet want of me
into a place that would never be new again.
Now an economy of nostalgia
for what never was makes some ghosts rich.
I own immense educational debt and too many
hypotheticals stacked like steak dinners,
warm and waiting with richness.
So how is it I can move these ocean limbs
to leave this bed each day.
And how did I even learn the shape
of tenderness, but in the two sweet hoods
over mud-wanting eyes. If I were
the first. Or the second. Or never.

Irrefutable Evidence

It's true. The people you love consume
glasses of orange juice when you're not there,
arms and hearts moving thoughtlessly, intact.

It will be the wind eating stones, horses, an ice cube
knocking against teeth that convinces you,
perhaps light on the hairs of the tomato vine.

The heads of bourbon roses float in a crystal bowl
inside a city, where you are both mayor
and black silk-stocking caught in a tree.

Tonight, a nearby wood is thinking of you.
Soon the streetlamps will begin to switch on,
for those who attended the burial have all gone home.

The Projected Future Has Been Cancelled

But my God, those ghosts were beautiful: the elegant waistlines of our children,
my hands reaching down to cradle your feet.

What comes after is water in cups, the wide world gone gray.
If it were springtime in a more tender decade, letters would be awaiting us.

But with pixels and hairs—we are learning something more. Your neck is gently damaged.
I am fully functional, completely like a sunset, insecure.

This amid the facts of a stripped mattress. And if someone inquires, re: your moment,
I'll respond: a fire truck idling in the middle distance and mine: something about fathers,
something about home.

Left with a cheese called Celtic Promise, Big Buck Hunter, and the fisted light at noon.
But we are contemporary and we are gentle and without dignity, we are growing old.

And now I see that it was more like a hand under my tee-shirt, more like waiting in line.

Dreaming the Places My Father's Tongue Has Been in Summer

Those goddamn lonely moments when I address him in the orchard
of his blue eyes, I ask him to tell me one unwholesome thing,
and he deflects. I remember being the only one watching moon color

clinging to the shoreline (white hairs flat against my legs). Somehow
I knew what to notice about the heat of summer crouching in corners,
and there I found a good and satisfying fear. His rugged forehead taught me

to be incandescent with the promise of exception. And still I wish to speak
some loose sentence in the orchard, in the office, in the gliding car: *What is love?*
Is it piston motion? Is love a warm and quiet mouth? The further shore or exhausted arms?

So I have inherited his tiny throat, squeezing food like a fist. Now home
could be a folding of wings, some calculated sentiment. I remember his hands
holding a map like smoke, my body strapped in the backseat becoming the shape

of a girl, becoming the shape of a spare and exceptional girl.

Theorem

And if that, then
this: our lives will be
a willing tongue slipped
into the grooves
lining a smoke-soaked
Connecticut clapboard,
a small place we can't
afford. And if that, then
this: the heart is when
things turn purple—
specifically—the seep that starts
as you are driving somewhere
desperately and all alone.
And if so, then it's known
that we are destined
to grow into sorrow deserved,
into brown bone. Now I want
nothing more than to alert you
to the fact that you are perfect
exactly as you never were.

Adolescence

Pull the blanket of calmed bees up to your throat.
Think about what it is you need.

In an empty room a boy clasps his hands together.
He sees the future: a small boat lodged among reeds.

Tonight a wordless want is in the air. Red hearts
grow heavy, bending branches in the grove.

A cold moon stares at itself in the river.
No meats have been cured for the inevitable winter.

A young grief spreads her wings and flies away; you
let out a small cry and prepare for the others to go.

But I Will Carve Your Name Into Any Tree Like I Am Fourteen And Do Not Know What Darkness is Possible

My arm wrapping your head like a sable cuff.
The sky in its indigo indifference.

> Our parents quiet pigeons
> > bringing back the daily news.

The cork is slid thoughtlessly from the green throat of bottle,

> and each day is placed atop the last
> like a ritual.

Small things have been folded out of being.

I address the wolf breath buried in the side of my mother:

> you crouch, you mingle, make a lovely menace by degree.

I tell my mother I did not kiss the girl with wide shoulders in New Jersey.
I did not fuck Stephan along the Westside Highway.

And what are we but our own legs and other tender organs,

expanding smooth as bay water out into the old dead summer air.

Knickerbocker Avenue

And the log of our days read like this: forearm, tongued calf, Billie Holiday's hands.
And evening came up like a sneeze each time.

We knew the scent of shaved skin and wet wool. The word *indefatigable*
somehow written on everything. The days born with pointed heads and tired eyes.
Each day cooked in its own slow fat.

We named places for what never happened there: Quiet Closure, Orgasm,
A Man Speaking Her Name Into Her Hair.
I dropped prayers on your body like birthmarks, darkening all
that was imperfect and trembling.

Toward where you might be now, I found a shard of bottle glass
and just one photograph. And the children on their wheels over wet streets,
the sneakers, the windows, books I still own.
The future remains uncertain as girls.

Three

Irresistible Empire

Not the house built but the aperture
of land before it was cut. Once

there was a stillness like that, of dust
and light in paneled rooms.

Then a blue flame lit under milk.
Now it is birds. Now it is the risk

and wish moving in a body
that can scatter. Here the appetite

is bread thrown into water.
It will not learn to dissolve.

There are moments of trust
and there are intricate channels

of fatigue. A strange dawn works
on us now. Open it. Nothing else will do.

Stand By Your Man

Keep it clean as the chrysanthemum bloom of skin,
she told me. Speaking for the first time of my body,
where all thinness gathers at the wrist.
The sad part about happy endings is there's nothing to write about,
and she was right as night dropping in now on its fleshy cloud legs.
But still: bless the obsidian thing. And bless you here with me,
your hounded sparkling eyes, the glass necessities, delicate fingers done up
to shine. We have the cardamom sky and this one impeccable hour.
So Virginia Pugh can rest her exhausted heart and all her intelligent pain.

Sisters

If the night is damp, the wind will be smooth, stretched tight as skin over ribs.
If the night is clear and cold and turns to glass against a warm hand,
then I am an empty room where you once lived for just a short time.

If it is raining the swans gather beneath the bridge, dirty loaves in dark water.
Winter is raging in the garden, while this new world tastes of something menstrual
and cool. And if the seasons have settled, the wanting has been shut up in a box,

and sent away like ill-behaved sons. In an office, in a shallow brown drawer,
resides all of our yellowed significance. And here is the rhythm of a red light
blinking, the hot pulse of it caught in your hair.

Your Mother: Franz Kafka. My Father: A Hole Ripped in the Night.

When we met the hot song on your lips did not stand a chance
against the things I wanted to do to you, things that would damage

your person in delicate, irreparable ways. Now Wednesday
evenings are filled with quiet cars caressing the curb, dead voices of distant

children, some hot hum of normalcy. And the dress I wore
was this weary world. But in the future of our inevitability,

there are broken shopping carts. And you have buried the cat's bones in the yard,
so when I move to admire the gazebo, to touch the unruly lavender bush

and break its fruit to pieces, I cross a delicate death and arrive unscathed.

Far as Fieldstones from Our Heads

The crow-crouched season will return, that slowness coming back like old cold.
In the ideas of our fathers, where there are small hands, smaller than expected,
and in a lover, it is something that begins in the wrist and ends twelve years from now.

If my mother gave me anything, it was the permission to rain.
So listen to me when I say your essence is green and gold and slight,
and remains tucked away from me. And your smell: sweet dead sun, a yearn.

What's in the white hairs of denim cutoffs telling my summer legs something.
Now this poem is inviting you in, with your tired jaw gone humming,
with your degrees of delicacy to which the red world remains indifferent still.

Intimacy

At dusk, a rabbit quick in the yard like liquor, and once,
how Josh called me the most beautiful thing to ever perch naked on his brown chair.

That summer I learned loving oneself is difficult, and it takes a very long time.
But the prize for this is two bodies and how they will betray us—
easily at first, and then with vigor and memories.

It is moments like this that I wonder: did my mother wear skirts as a child?
Where did she place her knees?
The cough and the wine mean different feelings at different times.
The lilies mean only one specific word.

Bent over Josh's unmade bed I learned to be kinder to my body.
The skin loose from my mother's naked knee saying: hold even this hurt close, too.

Soft Volcano

Thickly modern, that old sun rises like a cat certain of its own verisimilitude.

                                        We have done little harms to each other,

and we shared soup when the moment was right.

Remember the nights we animalled until full dawn,

                                        got vicious and chomped the starlight,

            the gashed darkness spread like sick around this place.

I still stop dead for the marvelous mouth of you,

                            even if our skins droop and waver,
cleft and lift at inopportune times.

                Now the scent of baby heads, of mother mouths and dishes.

        Good morning, little headache of this life I inadvertently chose.

                            I wish to make a ravishing of you.

Let's stomp around without apology, surrender again today.

Wedding Season

The red shoes, the cheeses, a rabbi.
Traffic like a tiger.
The city bleeds a little orange,
but weather never means to disappoint.
A sudden shout
as we remember ourselves, our age.
They got the fonts all wrong,
though pressed into wet paper.
The sun bellies up hopelessly.
Puffed lips should not be ignored
in the afternoon, and later
you move into me like night water,
and I feel the heat of blown glass inside.
The girls wear flower rings in their hair,
and sink sharp heels into compliant grasses.
The men drink like they are not children at all.

In Every Lonely Place, An Alter

A Milky Way mouth on the horizon, and flags we thought forgotten a few wars ago.
Out here we grow blister thick with jam and cornbread, drive around all day,
little steel animals gliding along the curves of old land.
No homes for miles, but in each clapboard square,
does a woman rest, callous, beaten, and sexed.
A crisp snakeskin left on the porch means some sort of progress.
While the whole county puts on a dress of orange light every so often,
and parades around big cheeked and unembarrassed.

Sheriff Teeth

Your father was a man made of chest: big as a country,

wrapped in starch and seams. Now suddenly September

and trees drop their leaves like thick skirts made unnecessary

by a quick lust and obligation. Things are changing here.

Your father is dead. And the rose bushes are leaking

their manicured redness into the streets. So far gone

is the evening your parents sat drinking cold tea

on brown chairs that swallowed their bodies

as we were passing through, just trying to lose

our virginity. Now our friends have children who will

have children and then some. And this has nothing

to do—and everything—with how much our fathers

resemble our selves. How much we desire them to.

Green Hour

An exquisite doubt rests on the table,
along the cooled teakettle, among spoons
still cradling their wet. Everything fragile
will meet me in the morning
when new light makes this place glass
hard again. Until then, let me be
comprehensive about weighing the risks.
Let me wake by birdsong, travel
like a lone hound—all tongue and fur
and tired. Let me perform the essential
tasks one must. You are the rust gathering
like new sun, but heavy dirty and alone.

Small Rooms

My want, like yours, is a thimble, a thick-blooded thing and this life,
a small fawn-legged accident, inevitable to fall.

What bereaves is what betters, and what I love about you is what I love
about snake anatomy, the vocative, blue air in an empty sky.

Tomorrow we will have to invent with the rudiments of September,
with nothing but pearls of navy and wood. Today my eyes are wild

for a skintight home. And if you play innocent, I'll play the dog-eared world—
sultry and caustic, too. Living is simple as licking the knifepoint clean,

as rising each day without forgetting. I believe the crust along the edge
of things is beautiful in its gathering, and I am far from where I am going, just now

learning to bend, toward better. The soft space inside instruction, and I want for you
to know this ravaged world well. Again my body is aching. You enter as water does.

Where God Was Not

We have no barn and therefore no swallows.
Though we could have raised children here once.
Today the mouth of the garden leaks a little green
onto the sidewalk unembarrassed.
What a complicated life this is.

*

A lone man lights a cigar in the doorways at dusk. The damasks grow cold inside.
Soon he will swaddle his mother in bent back, in colorlessness, in new smells.
That horizon remains.
The milk and butter crusted in old crumbs remains.

*

What will fill that place where the lip splits
and all the blood rushes out,
where the road became a cryptic curve of spine.
That celestial weather of yes.
A hunger like a thousand birdless wingbeats—
the air, the breath, and the deserted sky just after.

*

What other dangers will you step through tonight?
The hours baggy and gathering.
There is nothing mere about this.
I wanted like hot skin thumping around
the splinter caught within. That, and a tidy gold peace.

Convince Me Eternity

Six forty-seven a.m. is a bowl of bees on the tongue.
The part beneath sheets leans into the bit lip of dawn. The impossible
is less possible in the clavicle light of little February.
Though summer will come, and someone will run a tongue
down my bleak midwinter back.
For the foreseeable: forest of copy machines, lack called wallpaper.
Other tired hearts radiate broke heat on the train, through windows of cars.
What's past is throbbing, though I have not yet learned to calm
the muscle of wanting what I never had. Growing round-eyed, wine-toothed,
and I get old as the sun shoves off and the air goes black. Somewhere
the consistent surf is slicing sand beneath it. Somewhere there are children.
Obliterate a bit more until I'm among bloodstones in a field in Wyoming.
There is not one dignified thing about this life or that one.

Previous Winners of the Saturnalia Books Poetry Prize:

Telepathologies by Cortney Lamar Charleston

Ritual & Bit by Robert Ostrom

Neighbors by Jay Nebel

Thieves in the Afterlife by Kendra DeColo

Lullaby (with Exit Sign) by Hadara Bar-Nadav

My Scarlet Ways by Tanya Larkin

The Little Office of the Immaculate Conception by Martha Silano

Personification by Margaret Ronda

To the Bone by Sebastian Agudelo

Famous Last Words by Catherine Pierce

Dummy Fire by Sarah Vap

Correspondence by Kathleen Graber

The Babies by Sabrina Orah Mark

Also Available from saturnalia books:

Live at the Bitter End by Ed Pavlic

I Think I'm Ready to See Frank Ocean by Shayla Lawson

The New Nudity by Hadara Bar-Nadav

The Bosses by Sebastian Agudelo

Sweet Insurgent by Elyse Fenton

The True Book of Animal Homes by Allison Titus

Plucking the Stinger by Stephanie Rogers

The Tornado Is the World by Catherine Pierce

Steal It Back by Sandra Simonds

In Memory of Brilliance and Value by Michael Robins

Industry of Brief Distraction by Laurie Saurborn Young

That Our Eyes Be Rigged by Kristi Maxwell

Don't Go Back to Sleep by Timothy Liu

Reckless Lovely by Martha Silano

A spell of songs by Peter Jay Shippy

Each Chartered Street by Sebastian Agudelo

No Object by Natalie Shapero

Nowhere Fast by William Kulik

Arco Iris by Sarah Vap

The Girls of Peculiar by Catherine Pierce

Xing by Debora Kuan

Other Romes by Derek Mong

Faulkner's Rosary by Sarah Vap

Tsim Tsum by Sabrina Orah Mark

Hush Sessions by Kristi Maxwell

Days of Unwilling by Cal Bedient

Gurlesque: the new grrly, grotesque, burlesque poetics edited by Lara Glenum and Arielle Greenberg

Letters to Poets: Conversations about Poetics, Politics, and Community edited by Jennifer Firestone and Dana Teen Lomax

Artist/Poet Collaboration Series:

Velleity's Shade by Star Black / Artwork by Bill Knott

Polytheogamy by Timothy Liu / Artwork by Greg Drasler

Midnights by Jane Miller / Artwork by Beverly Pepper

Stigmata Errata Etcetera by Bill Knott / Artwork by Star Black

Ing Grish by John Yau / Artwork by Thomas Nozkowski

Blackboards by Tomaz Salamun / Artwork by Metka Krasovec